KRISHNA

THE ADORABLE GOD

OM

Om Books International

Krishna's Miraculous Birth

King Kansa was the cruel ruler of Mathura. Devaki was his sister. One day, he was driving back Devaki and her husband, Vasudeva to their house. On his way, he heard a prophecy* that he would be killed by the eighth child of Devaki and Vasudeva. Kansa was furious. He wanted to kill Devaki immediately. But Vasudeva stopped him by promising that he would hand over every child of theirs to Kansa, right after birth.

But Kansa's anger made him imprison Devaki and Vasudeva. "You will live in prison till I kill all your children—right up to the eighth one," said Kansa. All the guards in the prison were put on alert. Soon, Devaki delivered her first child. Evil Kansa rushed to the prison and without as much as a thought, dashed the child's head against the wall and killed it. "Oh my lord! Why don't I die instead of seeing my innocent children being put to death in front of my eyes," wailed Devaki. There was nothing they could do, but lament in prison till the arrival of their divine child.

After many years, Devaki was ready to deliver the eighth child. "Kansa is sure to kill this one too," said the scared Devaki to Vasudeva. "Do not worry my beloved! The lord is sure to show us a way," replied Vasudeva. And soon enough, there was a flash of light in the room and they heard a divine voice.

"Lord Vishnu is soon to be reborn as your son. Take him to Gokul, to Nand's house and bring back Nand's daughter to the prison," said the voice. The eighth child was born without a cry. All the guards in the prison fell miraculously asleep, and Vasudeva's chains let go of him on their own.

Vasudeva carried Krishna, the newborn, in a basket and walked towards Gokul in the pouring rain. "The river Yamuna's water is higher and there is such a storm. How will I cross it?" thought Vasudeva.

In a flash of a second, the river parted and Seshnag, Lord Vishnu's devoted serpent, followed them, shielding the baby from the rain.

Finally, Vasudev reached Nand's house and explained the divine reason why he was there. "Nand, my friend, I am here to leave my newborn in your care. Please give me your daughter in return," said Vasudeva. Nand handed over his daughter, who was brought back into the prison by Vasudeva. When the child let out its first cry, the guards rushed to Kansa with the good news that the

eighth child was finally born. "I will defy the prophecy by killing this child," said Kansa and ran to the prison. But, this time, he was in for a surprise! When he raised the child to dash it to the stone, the child slipped out

of his hands and flew into the sky. "Why do you kill me Kansa, when the one who is to put an end to you and your evil deeds has already taken birth?" said the child and vanished into thin air.

Kansa was perplexed and did not understand how the child could have been taken out of the prison, as there was nothing amiss in what he saw. "The guards were here. Devaki and Vasudeva could not have stepped out of prison. So, how could this child have been born?"

thought Kansa. But his fury knew no bounds that he had been tricked in some way or the other by Devaki and Vasudeva. "I vow that the child will be found and killed by these very hands," said Kansa and stormed out of the prison.

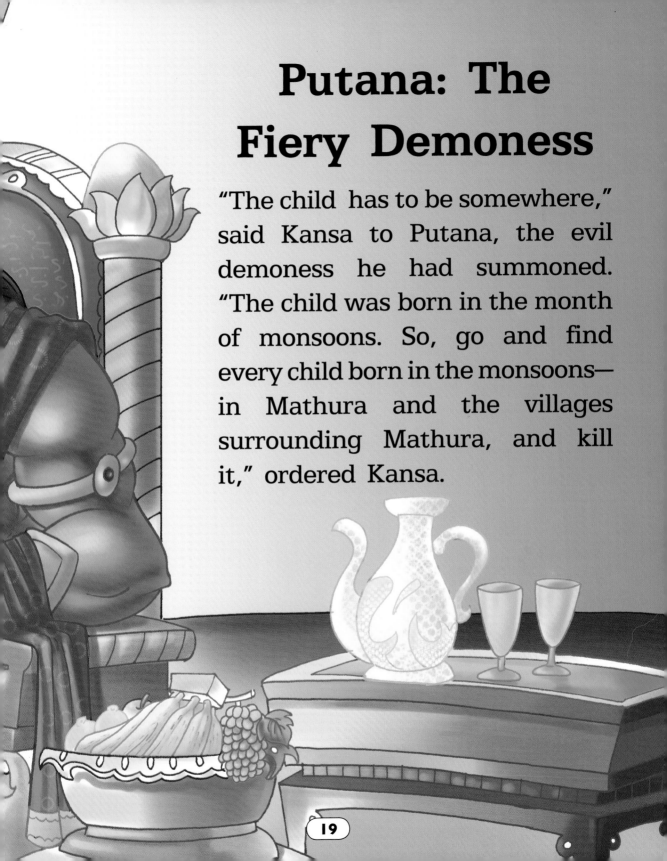

Putana: The Fiery Demoness

"The child has to be somewhere," said Kansa to Putana, the evil demoness he had summoned. "The child was born in the month of monsoons. So, go and find every child born in the monsoons— in Mathura and the villages surrounding Mathura, and kill it," ordered Kansa.

Putana disguised herself as a lovely damsel and went from house to house finding the children born in the monsoons. Putana would ask the mothers for their children showing her desire to fondle and play with them. But when,

they would move away, she would quietly poison them with her feed and kill them.

Soon she reached Gokul. "Nand's son is just adorable," she heard one of the ladies telling the other. Putana made her way to Nand's

house and found Yashoda playing with her son. "Sister, can you give him to me for a little while?" asked Putana. The unsuspecting Yashoda gave Krishna to her and went to fetch water from the lake. Evil Putana tried to poison

Krishna. But Krishna bit her so hard that she died within moments of trying to feed him. When Yashoda returned, she found baby Krishna laughing and playing on his own, with an ugly demoness lying dead next to him.

Putana's brother Baka, was furious when he heard about his sister's death. He stormed into Kansa's court and said, "Your majesty! Give me a chance to avenge my sister's death!" Kansa was very sure that Baka would not fail

as he was one of the most fierce demons. "Go and kill that little boy!" said Kansa.

Unaware of the demon, Krishna and his cousin, Balarama, were playing with their friends at their favourite place—the banks of

river Yamuna. Suddenly, one of the friends shouted out aloud, "Look Krishna! Look there! Have you ever seen such a big crane?" Krishna was surprised at how big the crane was. The crane was no ordinary one. Baka had assumed the form of a crane to kill Krishna.

"Let us go near and see it," said Krishna. But his friends were scared of this strange creature, and decided to stay where they were. "Then I will go and look at it from close," said Krishna and walked towards the crane. When he was close to it, Baka—in the form of

the crane—leapt at him with his huge beak
and swallowed Krishna.

Balarama and the boys were shocked at
what had happened. Balarama ran towards
the crane to save his brother.

But Krishna, had transformed himself into a ball of fire inside Baka's stomach. He burnt the crane from inside. Unable to bear the heat, Baka spit out the ball of fire. As soon as the fire came out, it magically transformed into

Krishna again! Within minutes, Krishna caught hold of the crane's beak—one part of the beak in his right hand and the other pressed under his right foot—and tore it apart.

And, that was the end of Baka, the demon! "Krishna, it's amazing to see how you achieve such hereoic deeds!" said Krishna's friend. Humble Krishna merely smiled and said, "Let's get back to our game. That was more interesting!"

Baby Krishna Slays Powerful Demons

Even as a child, Krishna was very powerful. His divine birth made him achieve feats that no normal human being could even dream of.

Kansa sent demon after demon to slay Krishna. But none of them met with success.

"There! You are sure to die in the skies," said Trinavarta, who had lifted Krishna into the sky by appearing as a whirlwind. But Krishna assumed the weight of a mountain and pulled him down to earth, thus killing him.

Once, Yashoda left Krishna under a hand cart to join in the celebration of his birth. The hand-cart was Chakrasura, the demon, who tried to put his weight on Krishna and suffocate him to death. But Krishna gave him a strong

push with his legs. Chakrasura assumed his actual form and fell dead.

When Krishna was a little older, he would always be found playing with his friends. One day, his friends found an opening to a strange-

looking cave and were drawn to it. Krishna followed them. But the cave suddenly shut itself. It was Aghasura, the demon in the form of a serpent, who had kept his mouth open as wide as a cave!

"We are doomed," cried Krishna's friends. "Fear not my friends!" said Krishna. He tore open Aghasura's stomach and came out victoriously with his friends.

"The forests of Tulavana have such tasty berries," said Krishna's friend to him. "Alas, we can never eat them, as they are guarded by a powerful demon called Dhenukasura," he said.

"Dhenukasura will be no match for our strength," said Krishna pointing to Balaram and himself, and led all his friends to Tulavana. As they shook the trees for their berries, Dhenukasura—the demon in the form of a donkey—was awakened from his sleep. He rushed to the place the noise was coming from, and charged at Krishna. But Krishna and Balarama were too quick for him! They caught hold of his legs and hit his head to the tree, killing him.

Krishna and Yashoda

Little Krishna was a very mischievous and naughty child. Yashoda once caught him putting a handful of mud into his mouth. "Krishna, spit out the mud!" demanded Yashoda. But Krishna was adamant about not

opening his mouth. "Will you open it or should I give you a beating?" asked Yashoda. Finally, Krishna opened his mouth. But Yashoda saw was the most magnificent of sights ever. She saw the entire universe in his little mouth! She could see the planets, the sun, moon and the stars. Yashoda was shocked. But, within a second, Krishna made her forget the sight, and Yashoda was back to chiding him for his naughty ways.

Krishna's naughtiness continued with his stealing his favourite butter and milk from other's houses in Gokul. "Come, let's break that pot!" said Krishna to his friends, pointing to the pot hanging from the roof, which was filled with butter. All his friends made a formation and little Krishna climbed on it to take the butter out of the pot.

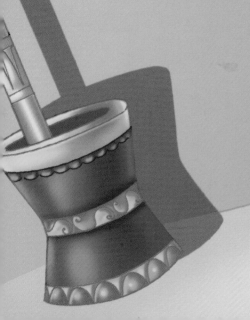

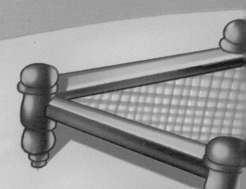

"Yashoda, it is impossible to live with your son!" complained the ladies. "Krishna's mischievous ways have to be stopped, or we refuse to send our children to play with him," said one of the ladies. "That's not all Aunt Yashoda! He stole our clothes from the river bank," said a young girl.

"Krishna, since you are continuing with your pranks, despite my warning you, I am going to tie you up to this mortar as a punishment," said Yashoda. But how could a mortar stop Krishna from his ways? Krishna pulled the mortar behind him and walked all

the way to the forest. When he was caught in the gap between two trees, Krishna gave the mortar a hard tug. Instead of the trees breaking, two divine gods appeared. "Bless us oh lord!" said Manigriva and Nalakbvera—the sons of Kubera—to Krishna. "You have redeemed us from a sage's curse," they said and rose up into the sky.

Little Krishna to the Rescue

Krishna's miraculous powers were always there for everyone to see. Once, the people of Gokul decided to offer their prayers to mount Govardhan instead of Indra, for the rains they received each year. Indra was furious with this and sent down heavy showers, flooding Gokul. "Save us Krishna!" cried the villagers. "We prayed to Govardhan because you told us to," said one of the villagers. "If so, I will save you," said Krishna and lifted mount Govardhan on his little finger. The entire Gokul took shelter under the mountain.

When the waters of Yamuna were poisoned by the presence of Kaaliya the snake, all the villagers ran to Krishna for help. "Krishna, my son was killed a few days back because he drank the poisoned waters of Yamuna," said one of the villagers. "And, our cattle have nowhere to

go for water, as the river is poisoned. Someone
has to kill Kaaliya," said another villager.

Krishna thought for a little while and
jumped into the waters of the Yamuna. "Your
brave son has jumped into the Yamuna to
fight Kaaliya," shouted a villager, giving the

news of Krishna's bravery to Yashoda. But Yashoda was far from amused. "He is no warrior. He is just a child!" she said, and ran to the banks of the Yamuna, crying.

However, everyone was surprised to see what emerged from the waters. There was Kaaliya with all his heads hung low, and there was Krishna, dancing on his heads!

Kaaliya's wives pleaded with Krishna for his life, and Krishna let him go with the condition that he would never come back to the waters of the Yamuna.

Krishna and Kesi

Kansa was helpless. One demon after the other was being killed by Krishna. "How are my most powerful demons failing in front of a little boy?" he shouted out in anger, in his palace.

"My lord! Do not lose hope. You have Kesi, who will never fail you," said his trusted minister. Kansa summoned Kesi and ordered him to kill Krishna. Kesi assumed the form of a horse and gallopped into Brindavan.

As all the people in Brindavan ran inside their houses seeing the wild horse, Krishna stood in front of Kesi fearlessly.

Kesi rushed at Krishna with great speed. Krishna caught hold of his legs and rotated him for a few seconds before throwing him a

few yards away—as if he were just a stack of hay! Kesi was unconscious for a short while. But, he soon regained himself and again moved swiftly towards Krishna neighing furiously, with his mouth open. But Krishna remained as calm as ever.

He thrust his left hand inside Kesi's mouth. Krishna's hand was as hot as an iron rod inside Kesi's mouth. Kesi was unable to bear the heat, and his eyes bulged out, before he fell dead to the ground.

As the people of Brindavan stood astonished at this miracle of a little boy conquering such a powerful beast, the gods from heaven showered their blessings on Krishna in the form of flowers.

Krishna and Vyomasura

One day, Krishna and his friends decided to play the game of hide and seek, near mount Govardhan.

Since it was mountainous region, there were lot of big rocks and caves around for the children to hide. Unknown to the children, Vyomasura, the demon had come there to kill Krishna.

"Krishna, it is now your turn to find us," said one of the boys. As Krishna began his count, all the friends scattered in the nearby areas and took their positions. But, evil Vyomasura, kidnapped one child after the

other without Krishna's notice, and shut them up inside a cave.

Soon Krishna turned around to find his friends, and found them missing. "Where are you?" he shouted aloud, but there was no

answer. Krishna turned around to see Vyomasura standing in front of him. Vyomasura rushed towards Krishna, but Krishna caught him within his grip and suffocated him. Vyomasura tried to grow in size, but Krishna would not allow him to move out of his grip. Krishna's powerful grip took its toll on the demon and he fell to the ground dead.

"There you go!" said Krishna pushing away the rock, which was shutting the opening to the cave. Krishna's friends jumped with joy on being rescued. "We were so scared Krishna," said one of Krishna's friends. "But we were sure you would save us," said the other. Krishna smiled at them and said, "Well, I caught you all at once. Didn't I?"

And thus, one more attempt by Kansa to kill the divine child was foiled.

Krishna Triumphs

Krishna's divine ways had reached the ears of Kansa. "It is time I call him to Mathura and kill him myself," thought Kansa. He sent an invitation to Krishna at Gokul. Nand was worried about his dear son's fate and pleaded with him to refuse the invitation. "Do not be afraid, father!" said Krishna to Nand. "Justice will always rule over evil," he said and proceeded to Mathura with Balaram.

There was a wild elephant waiting to welcome them at the gates of Mathura. Krishna and Balaram understood the evil ways of Kansa once they saw the elephant. Krishna pushed the elephant down, and killed it by pulling its tusks out.

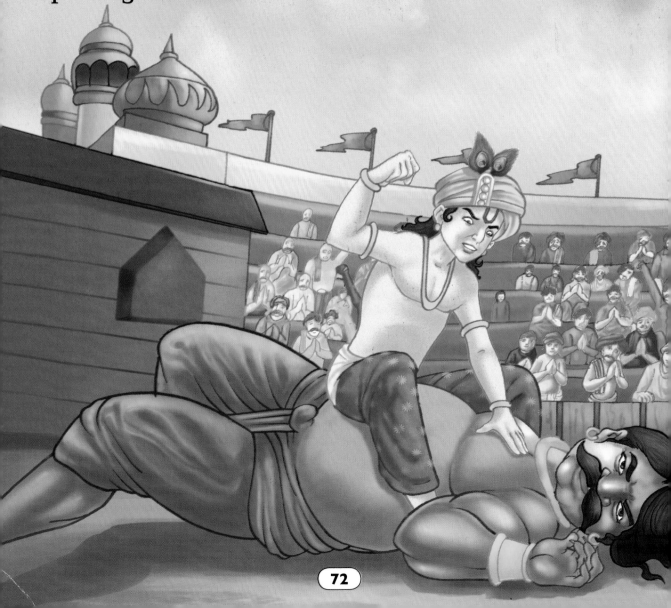

Finally, Krishna and Balaram proceeded to the amphitheatre, where Kansa was seated on a throne along with Devaki and Vasudeva. Krishna defeated one after the other muscled men in the duels that followed.

When there was no one left to counter Krishna, all eyes turned towards Kansa. "Krishna, you will now meet your equal," he

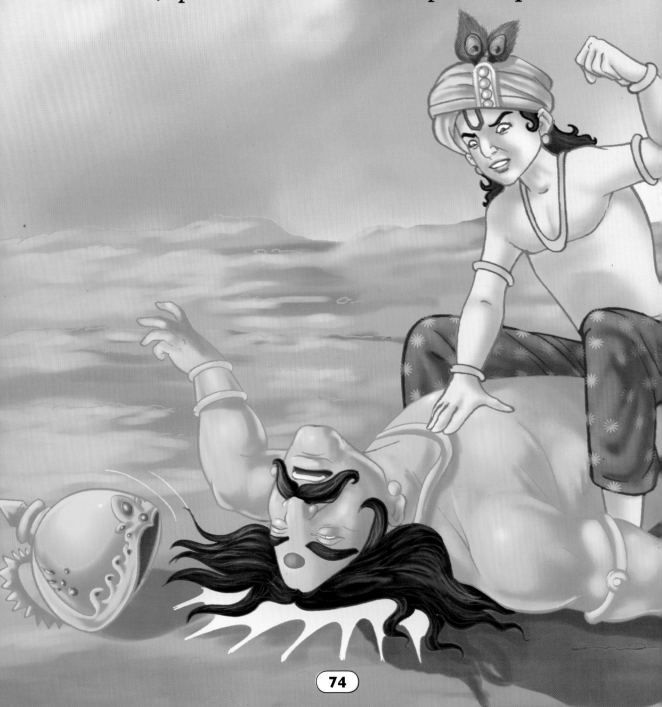

said and jumped on to the ground. Kansa fought with all his might. But Krishna knocked him down and killed him.

"My darling son!" cried Devaki, taking Krishna in her arms. "You have finally restored peace and justice to Mathura," said Vasudeva.

Krishna lived with them in Mathura, and went on to achieve impossible feats in his youth.

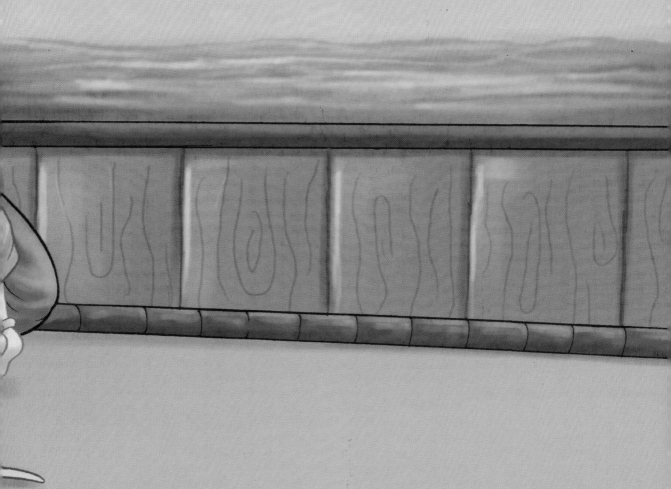

Mahabharata

Krishna's role in the Mahabharata is cherished by everyone—till date. His miraculous powers in saving the Pandava honour at every stage during the war; and his advise to Arjuna—which created the Bhagavad Gita—is known to one and all.

The teachings of the Bhagavad Gita are very relevant for modern day living. Krishna lives in our hearts, adored for his childhish pranks, guiding us to live life the right way.